Lead UP!

Equipping Today's Youth to Lead with Impact

Bernard K. Haynes

Lead UP!; *Equipping Today's Youth to Lead with Impact*
by Bernard K. Haynes
Copyright © 2016, Lead to Impact™, LLC; Chapter 9 & Appendixes © 2019

For more materials and information contact:

Bernard K. Haynes
Lead to Impact, LLC
bhaynes@leadtoimpact.com
www.leadtoimpact.com

ISBN # 978-0-9961945-5-6
For Worldwide Distribution
Printed in the U.S.A

Edited by: Shannon Rasmussen

Published by:
Lead to Impact LLC
3740 Falls Tr.
Winston, GA 30187

Table of Contents

Introduction

"The world makes way for the man who knows where he is going." Ralph Waldo Emerson

Lead UP!; *Equipping Today's Youth to Lead with Impact* contains 10 short, easy-to-read motivational messages that will encourage, equip and empower young people to lead with impact. Each chapter contains introspective questions to help young people formulate a working plan to live their best lives.

Many of today's youth desire to experience victory in life. They want to make a contribution to the world that makes an impact and leaves a lasting impression. The problem is they can allow the divisive voices of others, the distractions of today's social media, the diversion of life's busyness and the discontentment of the world's bitterness, to keep them from living their best life.

It is possible for young people to live life in a way that makes them feel alive and adds value to the lives of others. This book is all about what it takes to lead to impact. It requires commitment, consistency and intentionality. If you are a young person who is tired of the status quo, losing when you should be winning, following instead of leading or falling into the same tired ruts over and over again, then **Lead UP!** is for you.

Don't worry if everything does not happen as quickly as you want. Don't throw in the towel if you do not get support from the people you thought would support you. Don't think doing things differently won't work today because you failed yesterday.

If you are a young person who wants to live at maximum capacity, or if you are a mother, father, teacher, mentor, pastor, coach, youth leader, grandparent, aunt or uncle of a young person who you want to see live at maximum capacity, then **Lead UP!** makes the perfect gift.

Young People. Get Ready. Get Set. Lead UP! And Live Your Best Life.

Chapter 1

It's In You to Win

It's in You to Win™

"No individual has any right to come into the world and go out of it without leaving behind him distinct and legitimate reasons for having passed through it." George Washington Carver

When I talk about winning, I am not talking about hitting a last-second shot or scoring a touchdown on the last play to win the game. Nor am I talking about making the last move to win a board game or picking the five matching numbers to win the multi-million dollar jackpot. I am speaking of living your best life at maximum capacity.

The wrong influencers

You were born to achieve something significant that only you can achieve. No matter who you are or what country, continent or side of the tracks you are from, you have a specific purpose that no one in this world can live but you.

> **You don't have to be a carbon copy of anyone. You can be an original. If others won't accept you for whom you are, then it is their problem. Your responsibility is to be an originator and not another**

Marketing and branding strategies from companies across the globe have convinced young people to be who they are not or to buy things to be like someone else. Young people allow these powerful and influential messages to infiltrate their minds and tell them they must act a certain way, drive a particular car, live in a certain house or associate with a certain group of people in order to be accepted.

Do not fall into the trap of allowing the daily barrage of thousands of commercials, sale pitches and television programs to dictate your life. Do not allow advertisements to convince you that you do not measure up to the famous athletes and celebrities. Do not let the pessimistic words of others or your own negative inner voice convince you that you do not have what it takes to be a productive young person. Believe it or not you have everything within you to live a winning life.

You will encounter turbulence in life. People who said they have your back will walk away when you need them to have your back. Plans that you thought would work in your favor will all of a sudden fall apart. You study hard for the exam and still fail. You work extra hours but it still seems that you cannot get ahead. You try to do the right things to take progressive steps forward, but something always happens to stall your efforts or push you back five steps.

The key to winning

The key to winning is not letting past failures, people's opinions or current mistakes define who you are and what you can do. I read a quote by Michael Jordan, whom many believe is the greatest basketball player of all time that really shed light on what it takes to win.

"I've missed more than 9,000 shots in my career. I've lost almost 300 games. Twenty six times, I've been trusted to take the game winning shot and missed. I've failed over and over and over again in my life. And that is why I succeed."

Successful people learn to forge ahead in spite of failures. They don't allow negativity from their current situation to strip their self-esteem. They realize that deep within them resides the power to win and they begin to use failure as a means to succeed.

> **"What lies behind us and what lies before us are tiny matters compared to what lies within us." Ralph Waldo Emerson**

They study what they did to cause the failure and what they would do again if faced with a similar situation. They understand they cannot go it alone so they seek assistance from others to help them succeed. They seek out trusted mentors, coaches or advisors to help them deal with the challenges of life. They reason that success is possible if they stay in the fight and do not give up.

Seven strategies

In the course of my life, I realized seven strategies from their wisdom that will help position you to win.

1. Squash negative self-talk - When I find myself facing an obstacle that I am unsure how to overcome, I hear a negative inner voice telling me what I cannot do. When that negative inner voice starts its onslaught of negativity, I refocus my mindset and consciously decide to change what I think about.

Many times, we are our own worst enemies because we sabotage our progress with limitations and boundaries, instigated by negative self-talk. It is imperative that you make a conscious effort to squash the negative self-talk and replace it with progressive self-talk that speaks positively to your today and about your future.

2. Stand strong against your doubters - There will always be people who tell you that you can't do something. They will tell you that others failed and question why you think you can succeed. Some will even provide statistics that support their claims. Your doubters can ignite that negative inner voice that says, "What am I doing?" "No one will support me." Or "I should give up before everything falls apart."

> **"The pessimist sees difficulty in every opportunity. The optimist sees the opportunity in every difficulty." Winston Churchill**

Do not let your doubters' pessimistic attitudes and negative outlooks prevent you from living your best life. Let them see your life flow in creativity. Let them hear your mouth speak life. Let them watch you accomplish what they thought was impossible. Stand strong and let your doubters know you won't give in or give up.

3. Secure truth speakers in your corner - Surrounding yourself with people who speak truth to you is one of the best ways to help you face and overcome the hurdles you will encounter. You cannot do it alone. You cannot run your race in isolation. You need individuals in your corner who will encourage and speak truth to your life.

Do not build your inner circle with individuals who only tell you what you want to hear. You do not need a 'YES' team. You need people who will let you know when you are off-course and who are willing to help you get back on track. Build your team with individuals who want to see you succeed and who speak truth to you even when it hurts.

4. Stay focused on your prize - Nothing great ever comes easy. Mistakes and failures are part of the process. The great athlete misses the key basket, fumbles the ball, drops the pass or strikes out to end the game. But what separates the average athlete from the great athlete is focus: a focus so intense even mistakes and failures do not stop him from pursuing his desired goals.

You will find that remaining focused on your goals and working to accomplish them will help you stay motivated during difficult times. You must constantly remind yourself that an unwavering commitment and consistent action will pay off, and the hardships are part of the process of reaching your prize.

5. Starve your fears - As soon as you start to pursue your dreams, fear shows its ugly head. It reminds you of your frailties and shortcomings. It whispers the ridiculousness of your venture in your ear. Fear tells you what is possible and what is impossible according to your credentials and experiences.

It is your responsibility to look fear in the face and tell it where to go. You cannot afford to allow the constant barrage of discouragement, diversion and discontentment to dictate your life.

> **"You can conquer almost any fear if you will only make up your mind to do so. For remember, fear doesn't exist anywhere except in the mind." Dale Carnegie**

You must starve fear's appetite for destruction by focusing on who you are and what you can do. When you starve your fears, you allow your faith to come alive. When your faith is alive, you possess the power to walk in victory.

6. Stop waiting for permission - Have you avoided going after your dreams because you are waiting for someone to give you permission to pursue them? If you have, I want to encourage you to stop waiting and give yourself permission to go after your dreams.

If you keep waiting for someone to pick you, you may miss your turn. Stop waiting for that special someone to pick you. Pick yourself.

Your family, friends and those connected to you are waiting for you to pick yourself and live out your dreams. You possess within you the potential to be a trail-blazer, a trendsetter and a real difference-maker. The only thing stopping you is YOU. Declare out loud to the world and your inner self that, today; you give yourself permission to pursue your dreams.

7. Strive to keep moving forward - It is easy to doubt that you can achieve your dreams when trouble shows up. Every time you take a step forward, something happens to stall your progress. You sacrifice your time. You commit to doing better.

You make the necessary preparations to advance in life. But it seems the harder you work, the farther behind you get.

Your energy is depleted. Your enthusiasm is drained. You just want to quit and throw in the towel, but you know there is a dream that resides deep within you and you can't let go. You must live it out. You must endure to the end. You must dig deep, stir up your gift and activate your vision.

Personal Application Questions:

1. Do you believe you have everything within you to live a winning life? Why or why not?

_____

_____

_____

_____

_____

2. List the challenges you are facing that make you want to run and hide?

_____

_____

_____

_____

_____

3. How can you gain victory over the challenges you listed?

_____

_____

_____

_____

4. What person or persons can you trust to walk with you in life during the good and bad times? How can they help encourage you to live your best life?

_____

_____

_____

_____

5. Young people live with different pressures: spiritual, physical, mental, relational, social or financial handicaps that can limit their effectiveness. These pressures can leave them disappointed, discouraged and discontented, never living to their full potential. Listed below are key areas in life that young people struggle with. Discuss in detail what you need to do differently or improve in each area to overcome the pressures in order to live your best life.

A. Relationship with your parents or guardians:

_____

_____

_____

_____

B. Relationship with your family and friends:

_____

_____

_____

_____

C. Finances:

_____

_____

_____

_____

D. Physical health:

_____

_____

_____

_____

E. Work, Career or School:

_____

_____

_____

_____

F. Thought life:

_____

_____

_____

_____

G. Social life:

_____

_____

_____

_____

"If you accept the expectations of others, especially negative ones, then you never will change the outcome. " Michael Jordan

Chapter 2

Excuses are not Accepted

Excuses are not Accepted

"Nobody can make you feel inferior without your consent." Eleanor Roosevelt

Too many people have a habit of making excuses for their circumstances. They blame everything and everyone for their situations. Their parents let them down, their friends treated them unfairly, the government failed them, and the list of excuses goes on.

Excuses are self-built roadblocks that keep you from achieving what is possible. Until you stop making excuses, your goals are just stagnant dreams. Stagnant dreams do not produce results. When you become serious about making a real commitment to achieve goals, you will eliminate the excuses and get the job done.

Listen to the bumblebee

Did you know scientists once thought the bumblebee should not be able to fly? Did you know that the bumblebee did not listen to the doubters or naysayers?

Scientists' beliefs were based on its size, weight and body shape in relation to the total wingspan: a flying bumblebee is scientifically impossible. The bumblebee, ignorant of scientific input, decided to fly anyway.

The Effect of Excuses
- Excuses sidetrack you from realizing your dreams.
- Excuses silence your leadership voice.
- Excuses suppress you from living your values.
- Excuses sabotage your vitality.

Like the bumblebee, you and I can't afford to let the negative words of others and the cynical reports from the media deter you from going after your dreams.

Turn a deaf ear to the pessimistic words spoken by discouraged and discontented people. Ignore the stings of negative input and discouraging thoughts and replace them with positive input and empowering thoughts. If you do, you will position yourself to achieve things no one else thinks are possible!

What motivates you?

What I truly love about the bumblebee is his motivation to accomplish his purpose, in spite of what scientists and others once believed. What truly motivates you? Do you have dreams and goals that motivate you to live a life of excellence in your family, school, health, finances, relationships and activities?

There are thousands of people who have great goals and well-thought-out plans but who never achieve anything of significance. They lack the motivation to make their dreams a reality. You and I need the kind of motivation I read about in an article by Randy Slechta. "Motivation supplies you with the courage to look at yourself in the mirror and realize that you can achieve more than you have," he says. "It drives you to be better than you ever have before, propelling you to great heights of success."

When you are motivated to achieve your dreams, you will develop and implement powerful goals that motivate you, no matter what the cost. Real motivation from within provides you with the internal fortitude to tackle any obstacles in your path.

> **Excuses young people make for not living up to their full potential:**
>
> - I don't believe I can do it.
> - I don't have enough time.
> - I don't have enough money.
> - I didn't have my father in my life.
> - I don't have the right experience.
> - I am too young.
> - I didn't come from the right family background.
> - I made too many mistakes.

Is your current place in life where you desire to be? If not, what are you going to do about it? Are you willing to do things differently and defeat the giants in your life with the tools at your disposal? You need to focus more intensely on where you desire to be and begin to make all the necessary changes to get there.

- You can't wait for the right person to show up in your corner to cheer you on.

17

- You can't wait for the right circumstances to occur to get ready.
- You can't wait for something magical to happen to motivate you to move.

Your eagerness to motivate yourself to move comes when your desires meet your dreams.

No more excuses

The bumblebee did not wait to get the approval from scientists. The bumblebee did not spend years studying how to fly. He launched out and flew. He did not wait 40 more days to study a manual or take a class on flying. He stepped out in faith and took a chance. The bumblebee went against the odds and did the inconceivable. Are you ready to do the same?

What excuses have you allowed to keep you from chasing your dreams? Have you told yourself that you are not smart enough to excel in school? That you cannot start your own business at a young age? Have you convinced yourself with your excuses that living a better life is impossible or out of your reach?

"One of the marks of successful people is that they are action-oriented. One of the marks of average people is that they are talk-oriented." Brian Tracy

You don't know what you can accomplish until you stop making excuses and do it. You cannot afford to sit on your dreams choosing to make the same lame excuses you made yesterday. You cannot continue to blame your parents, background, friends or society for the fact that your dreams have become nightmares. You must make life-changing decisions to move in a different direction.

If you want to grow to your full potential, you must learn to take full responsibility for your life. Accept where you are, learn from your past, make any necessary changes and take immediate action. It's up to you to make your move and stop making excuses. No one can do it for you.

Personal Application Questions:

1. What excuses have you made that have held you hostage from living your dreams? List your excuses.

_____

_____

_____

_____

2. What steps do you need to take to overcome the excuses that you listed?

_____

_____

_____

_____

3. Why do you continue to make excuses when you know you can do it?

_____

_____

_____

_____

4. Reflection: What one significant thing could you accomplish in your life within the next 12 months if you would stop making excuses and do it? How would accomplishing this significant thing make your life and/or family better?

_____

_____

_____

_____

"You can have results or you can have your excuses. You cannot have both."
Unknown

Chapter 3

Thinking for a Change

Thinking for a Change

"For as he thinks within himself, so he is…" Proverbs 23:7

Has your negative thinking kept you from living your best? Does negative thinking keep reminding you of the failures and mistakes of yesterday?

Roger Bannister's story

Several years ago, I read a powerful inspirational story about Roger Bannister. Roger Bannister was the first runner to break the 4-minute mile. Before he broke the record, it was widely believed to be impossible for a human to run a mile in under four minutes. It was believed that the 4-minute mile was a physical barrier that could not be broken because of the significant damage it could cause to a runner's health. The achievement of a 4-minute mile seemed impossible to break.

Negative thinking can make you feel that you can't live pass yesterday's crisis, today's circumstances or tomorrow's challenges.

On a spring day, May 6, 1954, Roger Bannister did what others thought was impossible; he crossed the finish line with a time of 3 minutes and 59.4 seconds and broke what others thought was an impossible record. The barrier that everyone thought could not be broken physically turned out to be something bigger – a psychological barrier that could not be broken in the mind. Until Roger Bannister decided to break through the mental barriers, he would have never achieved the incredible record-setting feat.

Breaking through the barriers

So what happened to the physical barrier that had stifled runners for years from breaking the 4-minute-mile? Was there a sudden transformation in the human makeup? No! Did Roger receive some kind of super power that enhanced his ability? No! It was his change in thinking that propelled Roger to break what others thought was an insurmountable record.

When he broke through his four-minute psychological barrier, it released hundreds of runners to break through their negative mindsets and realize that it was possible for them to achieve the same.

I believe the same can be true in your life so that, when you break through the barriers in your thinking, it will not only lead you to overcome barriers, but it will inspire others to do the same.

Thinking for a change

I imagine that Roger Bannister heard an earful of negative and discouraging talk. He heard the media say that breaking the four minute-mile was inconceivable. He heard the doctor's reports that stated it is beyond human possibility. He heard the analysts say the record would never be broken. At times, he may have even questioned, "What am I doing?" Or he may have thought, "I can't do this." But Roger decided that he was going to fight through all of the obstacles and opposition and accept the challenge.

He had an unquenchable hunger and a relentless drive deep within that kept pushing him to go after his ultimate goal of breaking the 4-minute mile. His vision of breaking the record was so powerful that it would not allow him to quit or give in to the naysayers or his negative voice. His mind was made up and his will could not be broken.

The moment he broke through his psychological barriers, the once impossible record became possible. No negative reports, discouraging opinions or false barriers were going to stop him from achieving what he knew was attainable.

> **"We cannot solve our problems with the same thinking we used when we created them." Albert Einstein**

The best step that you can take in the pursuit of your goals and dreams is to change how you think. If Roger Bannister had accepted that the 4-minute mile was impossible, he never would have attempted to break through his mental barriers. He would have allowed the negativity and pessimism to dissuade him. He would have complied with the naysayers' and his negative inner voice. He would have consented to the dream-killing experts.

Instead, he decided to go after his dream. Just think of all the things in your life that are possible if you believe and take action. You do not have to be the most gifted, smartest or most talented person. You don't have to have all your i's dotted and t's crossed. You must be willing to study, practice and work harder and smarter than others. You must make the sacrifices others will not make. You must take a stand, think you can and move with the assurance of victory.

Roger Bannister had to not only believe he could break the 4-minute mile; he had to exercise his belief. To break through your personal 4-minute mile barriers, you are going to have to believe the impossible and in the famous words of Nike®, "Just do it®."

Personal Application Questions:

1. How do you see yourself?

_____

_____

_____

_____

2. How do you see the world around you?

_____

_____

_____

_____

3. Think about what you wrote. Why do you think you see yourself and world the way you wrote? Where did these thoughts come from? How have the thoughts shaped you?

_____

_____

_____

_____

4. What artificial barriers have you erected in your mind that has kept you from living your best?

_____

_____

_____

_____

5. What parts of your thought life are helping you achieve success?

_____

_____

_____

_____

6. What parts of your thought life are holding you back or causing problems in your life?

_____

_____

_____

_____

7. What must you do to think better thoughts to help position you to live your best life now?

_____

_____

_____

_____

Watch your thoughts, for they become words.
Watch your words, for they become actions.
Watch your actions, for they become habits.
Watch your habits, for they become character.
Watch your character, for it becomes your destiny.
Author Unknown

Chapter 4

Face the Fear of Failure

Face the Fear of Failure

"My great concern is not whether you have failed, but whether you are content with your failure."
Abraham Lincoln

Have you ever been so afraid of failing at something that you decided not to attempt it at all? Or has a fear of failure meant that you subconsciously sabotage your own efforts to avoid the possibility of failing?

"The thing you fear most has no power. Your fear of it is what has the power. Facing the truth really will set you free." Oprah Winfrey

Many of us are afraid of failing, at least some of the time. But fear of failure is when you allow that fear to stop you from doing the things that can move you forward to live your dreams.

The fear of failure can be linked to many causes For instance, having critical or unsupportive parents may lead to embarrassment or humiliation; peer pressure or not fitting in can lead to doing things that are detrimental to one's future. All of these, and many more, lead young people to fear failure in their youth and carry those negative feelings into adulthood.

Signs of Fear of Failure

There is a lot in your life that can frighten you if you let it. "What ifs" can pile up in your life to the point where your fear is too heavy a load to carry. The Fear of failure can be so debilitating and crippling that it keeps you from progressing to reach your potential.

You might experience some of these symptoms if you have a fear of failure:

- Fearing rejection from others that gives a reluctance to try new things or get involved in challenging projects.

- Self-sabotage by procrastinating, making excuses or a failing to follow through with goals.

- Low self-esteem or self-confidence that causes an individual to use negative statements such as "I'll never be good enough to make the team," or "I'm not smart enough to pass the class."
- Complacency and comfort keeps you bound from stretching yourself beyond status quo.

The wonderful thing about failure is that it's entirely up to you to decide how to look at it. You can choose to see failure as "the end of the world," or as proof of just how inadequate you are. Or you can look at failure as an incredible learning experience to help you grow.

Every time you fail at something, you can choose to look for the lesson you are meant to learn and move forward. Or you can choose to have a pity party and stay where you are. These lessons are very important; they are how you grow, and how you keep from making the same mistake again. Failures stop us only if we let them.

Don't listen to the lies

The fear of failure distracts us with a critical voice that says things like; "I'll never succeed at living my dreams, so why try?", "People will laugh or talk about me." Or "I am a failure." The fear of failure convinces you to listen to those negative voices and lead a smaller life.

If you continue to listen and believe the lies that the fear of failure presents, you will miss accomplishing some great things. If you are listening to the hindering voice of the fear of failure, then it is time to reject it. You don't have

> "The brave man is not he who does not feel afraid, but he who conquers that fear." Nelson Mandela

to live another day in bondage to it. You don't have to put your dreams on hold because of it. You can live with the assurance that, even through failure, success is still possible.

Overcoming the grip of the fear of failure is not going to be easy. The lure of staying where you are is powerful. Preceding forward presents danger. It requires doing something you have never done before, going in a different direction and moving without all the answers.

The negative thoughts of fear will ring loud like a rock band at a concert. Every time you attempt to move forward, the decibels of the fear of failure increase. The closer you move towards overcoming the fear of failure, the more complacency and stagnation will pull you back.

Many people limit themselves and do not achieve a fraction of what they are capable of achieving because they fear failure. You do not have to spend another second, minute, hour, day, week, month or year held hostage by the fear of failure. Today, you can experience everything that awaits you. Take a leap of faith. Jump off the edge and live out your dreams even in the face of fear.

> **"My great concern is not whether you have failed, but whether you are content with your failure." Abraham Lincoln**

Implement the six steps below and face the fear of failure and move forward to get the results you desire.

Six steps to help you face the fear of failure.

1. **Identify past failures.** Make a list of your past failures. This is difficult, but it helps you confront your past failures in a real way. You cannot change what happened in the past, but you can learn and grow from it.

If you do not honestly identify your past failures and their causes, the chances of moving forward will be limited. You will stumble through life and fumble opportunities for success if you keep repeating the same mistakes. When you take the time to seriously identify your failures and their causes, you position yourself for success.

Identify at least (2) past failures.

_____

_____

_____

_____

_____

_____

2. Understand that failure happens. Thomas Edison, one of the world's greatest inventors, understood that failure happens. He said, "I have not failed 700 times. I have not failed once. I have succeeded in proving that those 700 ways will not work. When I have eliminated the ways that will not work, I will find the way that will work."

Even the best leaders in the world have gone through several instances of failure. Failing is a part of life. When failure happens, identify the root cause, deal with it and move on.

What were the root causes of your past failure that you listed above?

_____

_____

_____

_____

_____

_____

3. Learn from past failures. The best thing about a past failure is that it gives you an opportunity to learn and grow from your mistakes and prevent the same mistakes from happening again.

Stop holding on to what happened yesterday. Let it go. Today is a new day and you have to approach life differently. Yesterday's failures are where they are: in the past. Stop spending time holding on to something that is gone. Learn from the experience and do things differently so you get different results the next time.

What did you learn from the failures that will help you in the future?

_____

_____

_____

_____

_____

_____

4. Count the Cost. There is a cost for not following your dreams. You don't know what is possible until you move forward with your dreams. You could be missing a million-dollar business, a full athletic or academic scholarship, a chance to travel the world and get paid or an opportunity to bless your family. Are you willing to pay the price?

What or who must you give up to pursue your dream? What will you lose if you don't give it up? What will you gain if you give it up?

_____

_____

_____

_____

_____

_____

5. Set a goal. A goal helps you define where you desire to go in life. Without a goal, you have no direction to your destination. Start by setting one to two goals. These goals should challenge you, but not overwhelm you so that you give up.

Taking small steps to achieve one to two goals sets you up for "timely wins" that will help boost your confidence. They will give you the motivation to keep moving forward and prevent you from overextending yourself by focusing on too many goals.

How can you focus on your goals rather than your fears?

_____

_____

_____

_____

_____

_____

6. Do it afraid. The fear of failure immobilizes you. To overcome this fear, you must act. Don't wait for everything to be perfect. Don't keep waiting to do it tomorrow. Don't wait for the fear to totally go away.

You must act now because if you do not, you allow fear to win. I know it is scary, but do it anyway. I know there is the possibility of failure, but walk by faith in spite of the doubts. It is time to be courageous and just do it. If it doesn't work out the way you anticipated, then do something different. But the key is to do something now.

How has fear of failure prevented you from doing what is important to you? How can your fear be turned into an opportunity to pursue your dreams?

_____

_____

_____

_____

_____

_____

_____

_____

"Thinking will not overcome fear, but action will." W. Clement Stone

Chapter 5

What Does Success Mean to You

What Does Success Mean to You

"Action is the foundational key to all success." Pablo Picasso

How do you define success? If you ask 10 individuals their definition of success, you probably will get 10 different definitions. Success does not look the same for everyone because the picture of success is different for every person.

A basketball coach might define success as winning a championship. A CEO might define success as leading the number one company in his or her industry. A high school student might define success as earning a scholarship to a major university. A musician might define success as achieving platinum record status. You can see from the above examples success is defined differently depending on the individual.

Success is possible

Success is possible for everyone. It is not distinguished for a select group of individuals. It is not based on your family background or what side of the tracks you come from. Real success is more than the accumulation of money, the acquisition of material possessions or the amount of personal achievements.

> **"Success is not final, failure is not fatal: it is the courage to continue that counts." Winston Churchill**

To have real success, you must have a continuing desire to become the person God destined you to be. Success, then, becomes a daily process. Earlier in my life, I defined success differently than I do now. At first, I thought success was making a great salary, driving a nice car, living in a nice home and working in a marketing position for a major company.

Do not get me wrong: there is nothing wrong with having any of these as a part of your success journey, but they should not define what true success is. If your success only consists of these things, then you have a very limited definition of success.

Success is a marathon

Success is a marathon, not a sprint. It is a process, not an event. Some goals may happen overnight. Others require more time, energy, and work. Do not get discouraged. Keep moving forward with your plan. Evaluate your progress and make course corrections.

Keep your goal top of mind and keep your eyes focused forward. Michael Jordan once said, "If you're trying to achieve, there will be roadblocks. I've had them; everybody has had them. But obstacles don't have to stop you. If you run into a wall, don't turn around and give up. Figure out how to climb it, go through it, or work around it."

Success is possible for everyone. It is not distinguished for a select group of individuals. It is not based on your family background or what side of the tracks you come from.

> **"The price of success is hard work, dedication to the job at hand and the determination that whether we win or lose, we have applied the best of ourselves to the task at hand." Vince Lombardi**

Success has been achieved by some of the most unlikely people. There have been individuals who achieved great success in spite of their background, education and experience. They were willing to put forth the effort and do what it took to succeed.

You can turn on the daily news, read the most recent news feed and observe individuals around you to discover that success is not just predicated on the accumulation of money, the acquisition of material possessions or the amount of personal achievements. If these were the only attributes to real success, then only people with fame and fortune would be successful.

We see the glitz and glamor of celebrities, athletes and CEO's and think that is real success. We see people around us who seem to achieve great success with marginal skills and abilities. It's the reason so many people search for a "secret to success."

They're looking for an easy path; a magic pill that will solve all their problems and release them from past pains and give them great success with minimal effort.

No magic pill

I have some sobering news for you.

There is no magic pill. There is no smooth, paved road to success. There is no special three or five-step plan that will give you automatic success.

If you want real and lasting success that will stand strong when things don't work out or when things fall apart, your definition of success must change.

I realized several years ago that if I wanted to have the kind of success that was not just predicated on the accumulation of stuff, my definition of success had to change. I wanted the kind of success that was built on becoming the person God desires me to be. So I changed my definition of success.

Success is becoming the person you are purposed to be, living positive values that guide your daily choices and actions, accomplishing the goals that give your life direction and sowing seeds that empower others.

> **"Everyone is entitled to success; we just have to make room for it. Learn to give up what is keeping you stuck and start moving closer to the things you want out of life."**

It is your responsibility to grow your potential for success so that you stand out to the world and shine the way you were designed to shine.

Success is not just going to show up at your front door in a nicely wrapped package for you to receive it. It is not going to be handed to you on a silver platter with all the trimmings. It is going to take effort and time to achieve the success you desire. Even if you have no idea of what you need to do, you can start by focusing on how to grow your potential for success.

Success is more than an idea; it is a state of mind. Although success is relative to each individual, the key to achieving success is the way in which you go about living your life and taking advantage of opportunities that come to you.

Personal Application Questions:

1. What inspires and motives you?

_____

_____

_____

_____

_____

2. Who is someone you know or admire whose work inspires you to succeed? Why?

_____

_____

_____

_____

_____

3. What is your definition of success?

_____

_____

_____

_____

_____

4. What actions can you take today to begin living out your definition of success?

_____

_____

_____

_____

"Life's real failure is when you do not realize how close you were to success when you gave up."

Chapter 6

It's Okay to Dream

It's Okay to Dream

"A dream is just a dream. A goal is a dream with a plan and a deadline." Harvey Mackay

When I talk about having dreams, I am not referring to the dreams you have while sleeping. I am not referring to dreams of winning the $50-million lottery or signing to play pro sports for $10 million a year. I am talking about a dream deep within you that is connected to who you are and where you want to go. You could also call them aspirations, goals, plans, visions or desires.

What are your dreams? Do you believe you have what it takes to accomplish your dreams? Do they keep you up at night? You think about them constantly. You know if you don't go after them, you will miss living your best life.

Go after your dreams

Anyone who has ever gone after a dream and achieved it will tell you the hardest part is getting started. That first week or two, or even couple of months, is exciting. But as you progress, things may get tougher. What was exciting in the beginning may potentially get bogged down in meticulous details and monotonous action.

A worthy dream is not something that anyone can easily talk you out of pursuing.

What started out as an exciting dream may turn into a nightmare. You hear others talk about how they accomplished and are living their dreams. They tell you about all the glamour and glitz. We see them post wonderful pictures on Facebook and Instagram. They tweet great messages of achievement. We see the stories told on our favorite television programs and YouTube channels. But many fail to tell the whole story. They leave out process.

The process refers to all the time between the origin of your dream and when you are living your dream. During the process time, a lot of people give up on their dreams. The road becomes bumpy and winding. People who said they would be with you leave. Doubt and worry infiltrate your mind constantly. No wonder so many young people and adults give up and walk away from their dreams.

I know what is to have dreams as a young person and adult, and I know what it is to see them fall away because I let things get in the way of going after my dreams. It is not going to be easy. You will have to put the time and work in to achieve your dreams. Talking and wishing about them will not make them happen. You must put forth an effort. If you come up short, that is okay. At least you took action.

Thinking about some of my dreams and the dreams of others I talked to, I realized six crippling dream busters we had in common. There are more dream busters than these, but I found these to be common denominators in many people that I talked to.

Seven dream busters

1. Living in a comfort zone. The desire to remain in your comfort zone is natural. But it causes us to jump on the *someday* bandwagon and push our goals and dreams to the side until another day.

> "Lack of direction, not lack of time, is the problem. We all have 24-hour days." Zig Ziglar

Unfortunately, nothing ever happens. Tomorrow becomes next week. Next week turns into next month. Next month leads to next year. Then next year leads to five, 10 and even 20 years of no action. Eventually, the life you wanted to live becomes a distant memory. You can't afford to fall into the trap of *someday* because it may never come.

You cannot afford to exhaust precious time and energy living in a comfort zone. Don't let fear, complacency or worry keep you locked in a comfort zone. It is time to break free and do life differently. It doesn't take a special five-step process or a magical formula. I discovered most of the time it only takes a slight adjustment in your daily life. The adjustments can be so small and minor that you miss them looking for something big and spectacular.

2. Failing to take consistent action. If you want to accomplish your goals and live your dreams, you must take action. You can have a powerful dream, a compelling vision and a well-written goals plan, but none of that matters if you do not take consistent action.

Consistent action is a reliable, dependable and coherent approach to daily living that aligns an individual with his or her life goals. This daily approach is not a system of habits, but a progressive attitude of pursuing your dreams even when adjustments and changes are necessary.

If you have spent time reading, researching and restructuring the perfect plan without taking action, you have wasted time. And though you can't get your time back, you can take action today.

Remember, it takes time to live consistently. It will not happen overnight. Don't get frustrated and quit when it takes longer than you anticipate.

3. Lacking focus. Lacking direction is like driving in your car to an unfamiliar destination without a map or GPS. You are in motion, but you are not getting where you need to be. You have an idea where you need to go, but a lack of direction will only waste gas and time.

We can all admit that sometimes, in our life's journey, we have lacked focus. You want to reach a goal, but your life's distractions keep interrupting. You implement steps to move forward, but the distractions keep pushing you back.

> **"Others can stop you temporarily – you are the only one who can do it permanently." Zig Ziglar**

To eliminate your hindering distractions, you must first decide to refocus your efforts on only what is important. Next, you must weed out everything that will not assist you in achieving your goals. Finally, prioritize your goals, take action and finish one goal before moving to another. If you find yourself getting off your life's target, refocus your efforts and remind yourself what you are trying to achieve and why.

4. Reliving the past. Yesterday is gone and will never come back. It is a part of your life that you will never get back. The only thing you can do about yesterday is use it to help improve your today so you can live a better tomorrow.

You can't achieve your goals for today if you are stuck on what happened yesterday. What you should or could have done yesterday is a fleeting memory. You can't rewind time and get a redo. Your moment is right now: do what you need to do. If you don't do it, then today will eventually become yesterday and you will have missed another chance. Don't miss your chance. Don't forfeit the time you have today trying to relive yesterday. Change your focus to the present, live your best today and tomorrow will take care of itself.

5. Listening to pessimistic people. Pessimistic people can drain your energy and kill your enthusiasm. They will constantly tell you what you can and cannot do. They will consistently see the negative side of life and remind you about it.

Do not allow pessimistic people to make more withdrawals than deposits in your life. If you do, you will find yourself living in the negative. It does not take long for negative conversations from discontented people to derail your life's progress.

> "Stop letting people who do so little for you control so much of your mind, feelings and emotions" Will Smith

You do not have control over what others say; but you do have control over whether you allow them to speak in your life. You have the power to walk away and reject their poisonous words.

6. Procrastinating. Procrastination can lead to laziness, robbing you of your will to get things done. Do not fool yourself: your actions and inactions tell you what you truly value.

Procrastination is simply putting off what you need to do today until tomorrow. For most people, though, tomorrow never comes. Procrastination is the enemy of progress and the friend of complacency. It leaves you with no drive, motivation or excitement to achieve your goals.

When you procrastinate, you put your vision, desires and goals on hold. You put things off under the illusion that you will get to them another day, or when you have more time. You make layers of excuses. You constantly postpone taking action. You end up always waiting for tomorrow.

Please be encouraged: you can overcome the hindering grip of procrastination. It will take a concentrated effort and an uncompromising commitment to transform from a procrastinator to a person of action.

7. Harboring a negative mindset. The way you think about achieving your dreams affects your success. If you possess a negative mindset, you probably won't make it. If you expect failure, it becomes easy to not try. If you live with fear, it is hard to overcome setbacks.

> **"A negative mind will always struggle to see and create a positive outcome." Ty Howard**

Negativity is like a weed: it will sprout when you least expect it. If you don't kill negativity from the root, it will keep coming back. It will come from people you thought had your back. It will creep into your spirit unexpectedly, trying to infiltrate your mind and fill your thoughts with doubt and discouragement. At the end of the day, negativity will block your focus and sabotage your future possibilities.

When you catch yourself speaking negative words or thinking defeated thoughts, immediately replace them with positive words and empowering thoughts. If you don't, your defeated thoughts and negative words will over shadow any attempt for a progressive mindset.

To overcome a negative mindset, you must refuse to think the same way. Renew your mind. Refocus your thoughts. Recalibrate your approach. When you make these changes watch your energy explode and your enthusiasm become contagious.

"If you want to make your dreams come true, the first thing you have to do is wake up." J.M. Power

Your Dream List

"Hold fast to dreams, for if dreams die, life is a broken winged bird that cannot fly."
Langston Hughes

Create your dream list. List some things you want to do, places you want to go, things you want to own and goals you want to achieve. This is your dream list! Do not be reserved and do not look at your current situation. Date each dream when you enter it and indicate one of the seven areas of life it pertains to (Spiritual, Physical, Mental, Financial, Relational, Social and Professional). Have fun!

Date	Dream	Area of Life

Date	Dream	Area of Life

Chapter 7

In Position for Purpose

In Position for Purpose

"The ultimate measure of a man is not where he stands in moments of comfort and convenience, but where he stands at times of challenge and controversy." Dr. Martin Luther King, Jr.

In our fast-paced, technologically savvy, consumer-driven, twenty-first century world, many young people have confused their cultural, social and traditional roles with who they truly are and who they can become. Young people have allowed consumer marketing and branding strategies from corporations across the world to influence what they spend their money on, where they spend their time, what they can do and who they can become.

Custom Designed

There are over seven billion people in the world. Of those seven billion people, none have your fingerprints and none have the material you were designed with. You are not a carbon copy of anyone. You are an original. When you were created, the mold was destroyed so that there would never be another person in the world like you. You are here for a purpose.

If you go to a designer to get a custom wardrobe specifically made for you, the designer will take measurements for your body size and dimension.

"The secret of success is to be ready when your opportunity comes." *Benjamin Disraeli*

He will take the necessary time to make sure everything is made to your distinct body proportions. If he has any problems, he will call you back to re-measure to make sure everything is properly sized. When the designer is finished, you will have a wardrobe that is customized to fit only you.

If another person tries to wear your clothes, they will not fit him properly because it was not designed to fit his body dimensions. It may look from a distance as though the clothes fit, but upon closer investigation, you will discover that they do not fit properly. The clothes do not fit him because they were designed to fit you.

The clothes were custom made for you and not bought from a department store rack where there may be clothes of the same style and size. You are not from the rack of a department store. You are custom-made with a unique purpose that only you can fulfill.

Repeat Champions

A couple of years ago I became curious about what it took for a professional basketball team to become repeat champions. I researched professional basketball champions over the last thirty-five years to find out what characteristics it took to make a repeat champion.

I discovered from my research that teams who won multiple championships had players and coaches that understood their position on the team. Each player knew what his main responsibility and role was in making their team champions. They made a commitment as a unified team that everyone was going to play his position at a high level every game.

> **Your life purpose is unique to you. No one else in the world can fulfill your purpose, but you. Whether it concerns an area explored by many or by only a few, what matters is no one can approach it the way you can.**

They decided to put the team above the individual. This took major dedication from each player to give up his personal success for the team. This kind of dedication and commitment took a major adjustment in their thinking. For some players, it took a transformation in how they approached and played each game. The players from repeat championship teams understood that when the team wins, everyone wins.

I learned from my study of these multiple championship teams that there were seven key positions (point guard, shooting guard, power forward, small forward, center, sixth man and coach) that must be performed with excellence in every game.

The more I studied these teams, the more I became enamored with their approach to winning. What I love about these teams is that not one player got outside of their position of purpose. If he did, he was quickly reminded that their ultimate mission was to win a championship. Each player over time learned to play within his purpose on the team. In other words, the point guard didn't try to be the center, nor did the center try to do what the point guard was purposed to do.

I realized that when everyone knows and understands their position and performs it at their best, they can achieve great results. The results for these basketball teams were championships. They became great teams that will always be labeled as great champions.

You don't have to have everything figured out. Life will throw you some curveballs. A purpose gives you a sense of direction.

You can start to realize your purpose now. You do not have to wait till you are older. Starting the process of realizing your purpose does not mean you have to lock yourself into a particular career

"Your life matters. You are here for a reason. Your job is to determine why."
Michael Hyatt

or job. It does not mean you have to do what the new job market predicts or you must have a static plan that cannot change.

Your purpose lives within you no matter where you go, what job or career you choose, what school you attend or what your circumstance or situation looks like. You may not know your purpose in its totality, but you can begin to fill out some parts. It is a process. You change and situations change over time.

Seven positions of purpose

After studying the key positions on repeat basketball championship teams, I realized seven positions of purpose for life. I matched the seven key positions of a repeat championship basketball team with the seven positions of purpose and here are my results.

1. **Coach – Communicates** the organization's vision to the team. You must effectively communicate your purpose to those that are connected to you through verbal and nonverbal actions.
2. **Point Guard – Concentrates** on leading the team on the court. You must remain concentrated (focused) so that you direct your thoughts, attention and actions toward your desired purpose.

3. **Shooting Guard – Consistently** needs to hit key shots. You must be consistent by having a reliable, dependable and coherent approach to daily living that aligns yourself with your purpose.

4. **Power Forward – Courage** to be the physical player that gives up his body. You must have courage to stand when everyone else wants to run and to act when everyone is paralyzed by fear.

5. **Small Forward – Confidence** to guard the opponent's best player. You must have the confidence and reliance in the abilities and talents you have to accomplish your purpose.

6. **Center – Character** to be the strong force in the middle. Your character is who you are when no one is looking and what you are willing to stand for when everyone is looking.

7. **6th Man – Commitment** to coming off the bench. You must make a commitment within your heart, mind and emotions that moves you on a direct course of action toward your purpose.

I want to encourage and empower young people to apply the seven positions of purpose to lead in their everyday life because, when they do, they will see powerful results.

Personal Application Questions:

1. Character

> *Your character is who you are when no one is looking and what you are willing to stand for when everyone is looking.*

1. What three character traits do you value the most? Why do you value these traits?

_____

_____

_____

_____

2. What three key character traits do you need to develop or work on? What steps will you take to develop these character traits?

_____

_____

_____

_____

3. What character strengths have you gained from a negative experience?

_____

_____

_____

_____

4. Reflecting on your life, tell about a time where you had to show right character in a situation when it would have been easier (so you think) to do the wrong thing?

_____

_____

_____

_____

"Be more concerned about your character than your reputation. Your character is what you really are, while your reputation is merely what others think you are." Dale Carnegie

2. Commitment

Commitment is the heart's direction that moves an individual past his emotions to live the purpose he desires. Commitment is tested by the actions of an individual.

1. In what ways has a lack of commitment kept you from achieving your goals?

_____

_____

_____

_____

2. What commitments have you struggled to keep while working towards a goal? What do you need to do to become committed through your struggles?

_____

_____

_____

_____

3. What are you willing to sacrifice or give up in order to live your purpose with power?

_____

_____

_____

_____

4. Reflection: Discuss a time in your life that you made a promise to commit to something, but after a short time your commitment fizzled away. What would you do differently?

_____

_____

_____

_____

"There's a difference between interest and commitment. When you're interested in doing something, you do it only when circumstance permit. When you're committed to something, you accept no excuses, only results." Unknown

3. Courage

Courage is standing when everyone else wants to run, speaking when everyone is afraid to speak, acting when everyone is paralyzed by fear, taking action in the face of danger, holding one's character and moral uprightness when everyone else is tempted to compromise.

1. What area in your life have you had to display courage in overcoming an obstacle or challenge? How did you overcome the obstacle or challenge or what do you need to do to overcome the obstacle or challenge?

_____

_____

_____

_____

2. How will you display courage and live your purpose even in the face of fear?

_____

_____

_____

_____

3. Do you feel that you show courage in trying times? Explain yes or no and give an example.

_____

_____

_____

_____

4. What can you do to stand in courage against an obstacle or opposition in your life that affects your purpose?

_____

_____

_____

_____

"Courage is the mastery of fear, not the absence of fear." Mark Twain

4. Consistency

Consistency is a reliable, dependable and coherent approach to daily living that aligns oneself with their purpose. This daily approach is not a system of habits, but a progressive attitude in living your purpose, even when adjustments and changes have to be made.

1. How can you become more consistent in living your best life?

_____

_____

_____

_____

2. What distractions are present around you that interfere with you living a consistent life?

_____

_____

_____

_____

3. How do you maintain balance in life while living towards your purpose?

_____

_____

_____

_____

"Small disciplines repeated with consistency every day lead to great achievements gained slowly over time." John Maxwell

5. Communicate

Communication is the outward expression of an individual's purpose to the world through verbal and nonverbal actions.

1. In what ways can you communicate your purpose to the world?

_____

_____

_____

_____

2. How are you going to communicate your purpose on a daily basis?

_____

_____

_____

_____

3. Have you discussed your purpose with your spouse, close friend or other trusted family members? What was their response? How can they help you in your pursuit of purpose?

_____

_____

_____

_____

"Think twice before you speak, because your words and influence will plant the seed of either success or failure in the mind of another." Napoleon Hill

6. Confidence

Confidence is the assurance and reliance in your abilities, talents and gifts to accomplish your purpose.

1. Give an example of a time you had to show confidence after being rejected.

_____

_____

_____

_____

2. Has a lack of confidence ever hurt you in achieving a goal? What can you do the next time if it happens again?

_____

_____

_____

_____

3. In what areas of your life do you need show confidence in your abilities?

_____

_____

_____

_____

4. Reflect on a time when you were confident that you were moving in the right direction and things seemed to be going well; then, suddenly, a tragedy, distraction or disappointment occurred that totally knocked you off-course. How did you respond? Were you able to overcome the tragedy, distraction or disappointment? What can you do if something similar happens again?

_____

_____

_____

_____

"Nobody can make you feel inferior without your consent." Eleanor Roosevelt

7. Concentrated

Concentrate is to direct one's thoughts, attention and actions toward a desired purpose.

1. What one or two strengths in your life do you need to concentrate on more?

_____

_____

_____

_____

_____

2. What are some of the biggest distractions that have kept you from focusing on your purpose?

_____

_____

_____

_____

_____

3. How can you maintain focus on your purpose despite all the distractions of life?

_____

_____

_____

_____

_____

4. Reflecting on your life – How has your lack of focus kept you from living your purpose? How has focus helped you in living your purpose?

_____

_____

_____

_____

_____

"Many of life's failures are people who did not realize how close they were to success when they gave up." Thomas Edison

Seven Poisons to Purpose

1. **Desperation** – You do things contrary to the character you need to display.

2. **Defeat** – You feel like a failure so you do not pursue your purpose.

3. **Diversions** – You become more attracted to the wrong things than the right things.

4. **Doubt** - You question your purpose in life.

5. **Delays** – You put off doing what you know you need to do.

6. **Discouragement** - You focus on your problems rather than possible solutions.

7. **Disclaimers** – You talk against the purpose you desire for your life.

1. What poisons have you allowed to distract you from living your best life? How can you overcome these poisonous distractions?

_____

_____

_____

_____

_____

2. Why is it important for you to overcome the poisons to your purpose?

_____

_____

_____

_____

_____

"Do not fear when your enemies criticize you. Beware when they applaud."
Ralph Waldo Emerson

Chapter 8

Your Values Count

Your Values Count

When your values are clear to you, making decisions becomes easier." Roy E. Disney

To become effective in your life's journey, you need to identify and develop clear and concise core values. Your core values are central in defining who you are, what you do and where you go. Once defined, your core values should guide you in every aspect of your daily life.

Define your core values

When you make a conscious decision to follow your core values, you cannot be easily persuaded to live against them. It is these core values that determine what is really important to you. The surprising thing is that if you ask most young people what their core values are, many would not be able to give you a solid answer.

"The chief cause of failure and unhappiness is trading what you want most for what you want now." Zig Ziglar

Some will give you a list of values, but they will not be able to prioritize them. They will give you a list that sounds spiritual or politically correct, but they don't come close to living them. In order to live your best life, you must have a set of prioritized core values that guides your daily life. Your core values should be:

- **Clearly Stated** – You should have a set of clearly stated and prioritized core values that guide your daily life.

- **Conscientiously Chosen** – Your core values should be in direct agreement with your purpose.

- **Continually Executed** – You should make a solid commitment to live your values daily no matter what is currently happening in your life.

- **Consistently Followed** – You are responsible for consistently living your core values on a daily basis.

- **Constantly Evaluated** – You should constantly evaluate your values to make sure you don't need to reprioritize them or make adjustments.

You may ask, "How do I determine my values?" **First**, you need to define what values are. Values are deeply-held beliefs that define what is right and fundamentally important you. They provide guidelines for your daily choices and actions. **Second**, to determine your values, start with the things that are important to you. List the issues, values, and thoughts that you think are important in making a great life. **Third**, pay attention to your life's experiences, family up-bringing and personal preferences.

Live Your Core Values

Once you establish your values it is time to commit to living them. Commitment to living your values is meant to be lived on a daily basis, no matter where you are in life. It is really tested by your actions and not your words. If you have a job, then you should value doing the best that you can do while you are there. If you want good grades, you should value consistent study habits.

> Your core values determine what is important to you. When you make the decision to follow your core values, you cannot be easily persuaded to live against them.

If you desire to be good musician or athlete, you should value training and practicing. You should value being a lifelong learner and making yourself better on a daily basis. Part of becoming a better person is staying committed to living your values at all costs.

In America we have become a society of instant gratification. If things don't happen the way we want, we easily give up. If someone does not do things exactly the way we want him/her to do it, we walk away.

Many young people and adults are committed to living their values just as long as it is easy and beneficial to them. Many individuals forfeit awesome blessings in their lives when they choose not to commit to their values because things do not go their way. There is no right or wrong way to document your core values and there is no magic number you should have. What is important is that you choose the right values for you and you live by them daily.

You should live by your values even when your life is in a season of confusion. You should live by your values when other young people are not living theirs. You should live by your values when the media and friends are telling you it is fine to live the way you want because other young people are doing their own thing.

"Strive for integrity - that means knowing your values in life and behaving in a way that is consistent with these values."

Because you commit to living your values, do not automatically think everything is going to fall into place. Don't think everyone that is close to you will support your efforts. Don't believe that you are not going to encounter some struggles. Sometimes the exact opposite happens.

Your life may get more chaotic. Things that once worked stop working. People who said they were going to be with you leave you hanging. That does not mean you give up. It may mean that you are on the right track to living out your values.

Once you establish your values and start living them, watch your life begin to turn in a different and more progressive direction. Don't get frustrated and quit living your values if it seems difficult, but keep believing and moving through the process.

Personal Application Questions:

1. What values have you had present in your life?

_____

_____

_____

_____

2. Name 5 to 7 important values in your life. Prioritize these values.

_____

_____

_____

_____

3. How will living your values affect your life and those connected to you?

_____

_____

_____

_____

_____

4. How do you expect to live the core values you established?

_____

_____

_____

_____

_____

5. Would you give up a job, friends, monetary gain, prestige and possessions to live your values? Why would you give up any of these things? Why might it be hard to give up any of these things?

_____

_____

_____

_____

_____

"Many people die with their music still in them. Why is this so? Too often it is because they are always getting ready to live. Before they know it, time runs out."
Oliver Wendell Holmes

Chapter 9

Vision Impact

Vision Impact

"The most pathetic person in the world is someone who has sight, but has no vision."
Helen Keller

The vision of equal rights for all people inspired Dr. Martin Luther King, Jr., to crusade for civil rights. The vision of a computer on every desk and in every home moved Bill Gates to start a computer company. The vision of greater discovery motivated George Washington Carver to discover over 300 different uses for the peanut. The vision of socially connecting people prompted Mark Zuckerberg to start the social media giant Facebook. Vision demands change.

What is vision?

Vision is a clear mental picture of a preferable future that gives an individual direction for his or her life. The person becomes so committed to the vision that he or she will pursue it despite any obstacles or challenges. It is the ingredient that launches an individual out of stagnation and into forward action.

Visions originate in the heart and mind of a man who is frustrated and tired of the way things are in contrast to the way he believes things could and should be.

I love talking about the power of a vision because it is vision that drives an individual to overcome the obstacles and opposition that he may face and do the work to make the vision a reality. I've experienced the power of vision in my own life and I know what is possible when you can see it and act on it. If you look within yourself and look out into the world, you too will know that you possess the greatest power in the universe: the power to see a vision for your now and your future and create it.

A person of vision sees what's possible and then takes the next steps to create it. Every invention, project, creation, and transformation starts with an idea, an imagination, and a vision of what's possible. History shows us that if you can see it, you can create it.

Live out your vision

If you have a vision, then you also have the power to live it out. A visionary person taps into the power of his vision and finds a way to move it forward while connecting others to it. But in order to move your vision forward and get others to follow it, you must be able to articulate and communicate your vision in a simple, clear, bold, and compelling way.

Helen Keller was asked, "What would be worse than being born blind?" She replied, "To have sight without vision." Sadly, too many people are trying to lead without a vision. A person of vision possesses two things: she knows where she is going and she is able to persuade others to follow.

Individuals can spend more time planning a weekend sporting event or what they are going to wear on a night out on the town than identifying

> *"Do not go where the path may lead, instead go where there is no path and leave a trail." Ralph Waldo Emerson*

what outcomes they want to see in the major areas of their life. This kind of mindset can lead people to wander aimlessly from day to day, week to week, year to year with no clear direction in mind. For this reason, I believe people should take the time to realize their vision to give their life direction.

Do you have a clear personal vision that gives your life direction? Does your vision cover every area of your life (spiritual, relational, physical, social, mental, financial, and professional)? If you answered no to these questions, you have some work to do.

The power of vision

What is possibly more satisfying than knowing the God of the universe designed you with a unique vision to impact the world? His vision for you is not a one-size-fits-all, but it is uniquely fashioned to fit you. No matter who you are, what country or continent you live on, or what side of the tracks you are from, you were designed with a specific vision that no one in this world can live but you.

I do not care who tries to imitate your vision; he will never live it as effectively as you. Even if he follows it step-by-step and word-for-word, he will never execute it the way you can. The tragedy is to live your entire life without ever living to the full potential of your unique vision.

Today's world

In today's stressful and chaotic world, many young people are busy moving at fast-break speeds hourly, daily, weekly, monthly, and yearly, but they still have no real vision beyond their current situation.

We can spend countless hours talking and texting on mobile devices, watching our favorite television or sports shows, Snapchatting, posting on Instagram, or checking our Facebook pages, but many of us have failed to spend the same quality time developing and implementing a vision that gives our life direction.

I realized several years ago that a clear vision was the missing ingredient keeping many young people from living their best lives. They experienced a lot of unnecessary struggle and frustration due to the lack of vision.

"There is no passion to be found playing small – in settling for a life that is less than the one you are capable of living."
Nelson Mandela

Conversation after conversation revealed that a lack of a clear vision in every area of life was the underlying problem causing frustration, fatigue, and failure.

It did not matter whether a person had a doctorate degree or a GED, was a business owner or a janitor, or was financially secure or not, the lack of a clear vision was the common denominator.

If you never realize your true vision, you will limp through life and you will miss living your best. You came into this world equipped with a vision designed specifically for you. It is up to you whether you realize your vision or not.

What vision provides

Unfortunately, many people don't live from vision. They live life like a builder who tries to construct a building without the proper blueprints. Because the builder does not have a clear vision for the building, he or she works from assumptions and guesswork.

Many people today operate in the same manner. They stumble through life allowing circumstances, events, and other individuals to determine their destiny. They often opt for mediocrity or the status quo, instead of living their best life.

I want to suggest to you that true success begins with a vision that supports every area of life. You must know where you are to get to where you desire. Vision is a powerful motivator to move you into consistent action.

A clear vision will provide you with:

1. **Focus** – A clear vision enables you to keep your eyes fixed on your desired objective. It keeps you from falling victim to distractions that may look good from the outside but are not the best for your life. Without a focused vision, you will live carelessly and without a sense of purpose.

2. **Energy** – A clear vision will energize you. You receive strength from the picture of where you are going and the incredible possibilities of living it out. The energy derived from a clear vision will remain at the forefront of your mind even when obstacles and opposition rear their ugly heads. Your vision becomes the spark plug that transforms stagnancy into action.

3. **Endurance** - Your vision not only gives you energy for the task but it gives you endurance to stay the course. Endurance is the ability to keep going even when things get tough. A clear vision will fortify you to push forward when you want to quit and gives you the 'staying power' when you want to throw in the towel.

People of vision make things happen. They accept responsibility. They aren't necessarily the most intelligent, privileged, or talented. They are clear, however, about what they want and they are determined to rise above any challenges, obstacles, and difficulties to make their vision a reality.

Can you begin to see your future? Write your future (dreams) in detail for the seven areas of your life. Refer to your dream list and answers to questions that you have written in the workbook.

---

7 Areas of Life to Focus:

1. **Spiritual – (relationship with God, prayer, Bible study, faith, worship, church)**
2. **Physical – (medical health, exercise, appearance, weight, nutrition, dental, vision)**
3. **Relational – (spouse, children, family, friends, forgiveness, love, honor, role model)**
4. **Mental – (education, reading, listening, creativity, thoughts, personal development)**
5. **Professional – (vocation, job, training, co-workers, employees, career, resumè)**
6. **Social – (activities, people, events, habits, dates, family outings, vacations)**
7. **Financial – (earnings, savings, investments, giving, debt, spending, budgets)**

Spiritual:_____

_____

_____

_____

Relational:_____

_____

_____

_____

Physical:_____

_____

_____

_____

Mental:_____

_____

_____

_____

Social:_____

_____

_____

_____

Financial:_____

_____

_____

_____

Professional:_____

_____

_____

_____

"Take the first step in faith. You don't have to see the whole staircase, just take the first step." Dr. Martin Luther King, Jr.

Chapter 10

Goals Matter

Goals Matter

"It must be borne in mind that the tragedy of life does not lie in not reaching your goal. The tragedy of life lies in having no goal to reach." Benjamin E. Mays

Are your daily actions bringing you closer to your goals? If not, do not expect things in your life to change.

It feels comforting to hear motivational speakers tell us how to achieve the goals that will make our lives prosperous. It's very inspiring to read books and articles about overcoming challenges in life to achieve your desired goals. All of these are great for encouraging and empowering you to set and pursue your goals. But the key to achieving any goal is putting feet to your faith.

The power of goal setting

Goal setting is an extremely powerful tool for accomplishing your dreams. Most people would be unable to give specifics if you asked about their goals and plans for their lives. Some would give vague and unrealistic answers and say things like, "I want to be wealthy," "I want a big house," or "I want to play pro sports." They would give general answers that are not goals but dreams desired by many.

> **What is a goal?**
> A goal is an aim, a purpose or a sense of direction toward which you move all of your energies, desires and efforts. Goals are the targets toward which you point your life.

Many people attempt to live their lives without a real plan. Imagine a football coach trying to lead a football team without a game plan, a builder trying to build a house without a blueprint or a CEO trying to lead a business without a business plan. All of the examples above perpetuate confusion because the leaders are trying to operate without a plan.

Planning is an essential part of setting specific vision goals. No successful business, corporation or organization was built without a plan. You may have great dreams and high expectations, but without a plan, they are just lofty aspirations.

I am not promising a magical formula that guarantees success if you read this material or fill out a goals sheet. Nor am I suggesting that, if you follow our 12 steps, you will have no struggles, and everything will magically fall into place in your life.

You must work to achieve your goals. You will make some mistakes. You may even fail at achieving some of your goals. Through every discouragement and disappointment, you must remain convinced that you can make your goals a reality.

> **Goals are not written in concrete or unchangeable terms, but they do give you a starting point and a destination to reach.**

Your written goals plan will help you to see where you are going, what changes you need to make and whether you are progressing toward the prize that is set before you. It is time to stop making excuses, procrastinating, and wasting valuable time and energy. It is time to start living your best life.

No one can easily talk you out of accomplishing a goal that is worth pursuing. It is a goal that rests deep within you, and you cannot let it go. Your focus becomes so intense that you will not allow current circumstances or others' opinions to hinder you. You will focus on your goals with laser-like attention because you understand that accomplishing them is part of becoming a better person.

12 simple steps to achieving your goals

If you are passionate about achieving your goals, our *Twelve Simple Steps to Achieving Your Goals* will help you write and implement an achievable goals plan. **On Your Mark! Get Ready! Set Your Goals! Live Your Dreams!**

1. Spend quality time alone developing your goals.

I advise you to get alone in a quiet place, away from the distractions of life, and begin to develop your goals plan.

Put away your mobile devices, shut down the computer and turn off the television. Tell your family and friends this is your set time for developing your present and future goals plan, and you do not want to be disturbed.

2. Define your goals in writing.

It is very important that you take your pen, paper and a Goals Matter! Planning Sheet with you during your quiet time. Record in detail the goals you desire to accomplish, because you are fooling yourself if you think you can remember everything that comes to mind in your quiet time.

When you begin to define your goals in writing make sure they are **SMART**: **Specific – Measurable – Actionable – Reinforcing –Trackable**.

We tend to forget things. Write down your goals! Written goals will bring clarity to your life.

Documenting your goals creates a road map to focus your directions. You will begin to see clearly what you need to do and how you need to get it done.

3. Create measures to success.

Now that you have defined your goals, the next step is to create ways to measure your progress. It is not enough to say I have a goal; you need a way to measure your progress. You define your measures for success by:

1. **Term (length of time)**

   - Short Term (within a year)
   - Medium Term (within three years)
   - Long Term (over three years)

2. **The Life Area** – spiritual, relational, physical, social, financial, mental or professional.

3. **Dates** – Start date, target completion date and actual completion date.

Adding these measurables to your goals brings a greater energy and excitement to achieve them. If you don't meet your measurables, please don't give up. You may need to make some adjustments. You may need to quit doing something one way and try doing it another way.

4. Define possible opportunities for success.

What potential opportunities do you know about that will bring you success? Is it a better grade, a scholarship, a new relationship or a great business deal? One technique you can use to focus your goals planning is to list three to five opportunities for success if you accomplish a particular goal.

Let's use the example of losing 20 pounds in four months. Here are a few things I would list as possible opportunities for success: I will physically feel better, I will be more confident and I will be able to participate in more physical activities.

You can list as many opportunities for success as you desire. Your list will become a huge part of your motivation to achieve your goals when times of discontentment, discouragement and doubt come.

5. Identify obstacles to success.

Now that you have spent time alone developing your goals, writing them down, setting measures to success and defining possible opportunities for success, everything should be smooth sailing, right? Wrong! Obstacles will attempt to distract and detour your goals plan. You may

> "There are no secrets to success. It is the result of preparation, hard work, learning from failure." Colin Powell

be able to identify some of the obstacles in the beginning, but some will come out of nowhere.

Identify at least three to five obstacles that you feel may prevent you from achieving your goals. List the potential obstacles that you have identified for each goal on your Goals Matter! Planning Sheet. Then begin your journey of overcoming them to successfully achieve your goals.

6. Break down goals into manageable action steps.

When you have a large goal that you want to accomplish, the best thing to do is break your large goal into smaller, more manageable action steps. If you focus on the enormity of the large goal, it can become overwhelming.

If you try to accomplish the large goal all at once, it can lead to frustration and burn out. If you break the large goal down into smaller measureable action steps, you set yourself up for success because you make your large goal more obtainable. It is much easier to break a large stone with several small strikes than one big hit.

If you have a large goal you want to accomplish, our Goals Matter! Planning Sheets include a section where you can list at least 10 smaller action steps with a begin date, target completion date and an actual completion date. Taking the time to break your goal into smaller, manageable action steps will put you on the right road to your goals success.

7. Identify people, resources or skills needed.

What resources or skills do you have or need to acquire to accomplish your goals? Who are the people you will need on your team to help you achieve your goals?

You may have to take an additional class or do an in-depth self-study on a particular subject to educate yourself on a new skill or re-educate yourself on an old skill. Trust me; you are going to need help from others. Don't be too ashamed or prideful to ask for help.

Dreams vs. Goals

Goal setting is like shooting a basketball: you may want to score a basket, but if you never take a shot – you only have a dream. The difference between your dreams and achieving your goals is Action.

You can't do it alone. You will need the support and encouragement of another person, as well as someone to share ideas with. Identify and acquire the resources, skills and/or people you will need and go to work.

8. Create new habits.

Setting goals is easy, but achieving them is a different story. You must find a way to implement a healthier routine to yield the results you desire. No matter how small or big the goal you set, you must create and implement new habits.

How do you expect to achieve your goals with the same tired habits you have failed with year after year? Nothing will change unless you make daily changes. You will continually fail to achieve your goals if your daily habits do not change.

Forming new habits is hard. It requires daily action. The promise of rewards will drive you in the beginning. But if you don't remain consistent and committed, after a couple weeks, your drive will fizzle out and you will return to business as usual. If you want your new habits to stick, believe you can change, and take action.

9. Take action.

Once you have a written goals plan, it is your responsibility to take action. You can't wait for the right person, time or situation before you take action on your goals.

You could write the most captivating, compelling and challenging goal possible, but if you don't take a course of action to implement your plan, your goal will remain just a wonderful dream.

10. Monitor your goals regularly.

As you move forward with your goals, you will need to periodically monitor them. It is important to measure your progress in order to make any necessary adjustments or changes.

> **"Always focus on the front windshield and not the review mirror."** Colin Powell

You may find you need to go right instead of going left, or you may have to extend the time required to complete an action step, or the overall goal. You may discover that your goal needs to be eliminated because it no longer aligns with where you want to go.

Monitoring your goals regularly will give you perspective on where you are and whether or not you are on the right course to completing your goal. The Goals Matter! Planning Sheets are great documents to regularly monitor where you are on your goals progress.

11. Reward yourself.

I don't want to make achieving your goals all work. Throughout the process, you need to implement rewards that follow key steps in your action plan. This will enforce your desire to move forward to the next step in accomplishing your big goal.

> **"How do you go from where you are to where you wanna be? …I think you have to have an enthusiasm for life. You have to have a dream, a goal. And you have to be willing to work for it." Jim Valvano**

Please make your goal achievement a fun and exciting process. Don't overdo it with rewards, because you still have a bigger goal to reach. Your minor victories deserve applause! You can establish other rewards as you accomplish more steps to your bigger goal. This recognition will enforce where you are going and provide an incentive to get the job done.

12. Keep moving forward.

Please know that when you take action, opposition and obstacles will try to take you off-course. They will come at you daily with a relentless arsenal, trying to hinder your forward progress. I admonish you to:

a. Commit to your specific goals path regardless of setbacks, challenges or failures.

b. Continually surround yourself with people who will encourage your forward movement.

c. Consistently show up every day to do the work necessary to achieve your goals.

d. Confidently operate in your abilities, talents and gifts.

e. Courageously fight through the temptation to quit.

"What you get by achieving your goals is not as important as what you become by achieving your goals." Zig Ziglar

List 7 Goals that you want to accomplish: (Write one goal from each of the 7 areas of life; spiritual, relational, physical, mental, social, financial and professional)

1._____
_____
_____

2._____
_____
_____

3._____
_____
_____

4._____
_____
_____

5._____
_____
_____

6._____
_____
_____

7._____
_____
_____

From the seven goals that you listed, choose three of them and work through our 12 Simple Steps to Achieving Your Goals. We have included three Goals Matter! Planning Sheets for you to write your goals and an example of a written goal of student who desires to achieve a 90 grade average in history at the end of the school year (5/25/2016).

Example: Goals Matter! Planning Sheet

Goal: (specific, measurable, actionable, reinforcing and trackable)

I earn a 90 or above average in my history class at the end of the school year (5/25/2020).

Measures to success:

Term of Goal: ___ Short-Term (within 1 year)   **X**__Med.-Term (within 3 years) _____Long-Term (Over 3 Years)

Life Area (circle one): Spiritual– Relational – Physical– Social - ***Financial***– Mental - Professional
Begin Date: _____**9/1/17**_____ Target Completion Date: _____**5/25/18**_____
Actual Completion Date:__**5/20/18**__

Possible opportunities for success: (What will you get from accomplishing this goal?)

1. **Improve overall GPA**   4. **Satisfaction of achieving an 'A' in history**

2. **Parents will be pleased**

3. **Victory over doubt**

Barriers to success: (Things that can prohibit you from achieving this goal.)

1. **Laziness**   5. **Not managing time effectively**

2. **Bad study habits**

3. **Spending too much on mobile devices.**

4. **Watching too much TV**

New habit(s): (What new daily habits can you implement to make this goal a reality?)

1. Study in 20 min. increments with a 5 min break in between. Study at least 1 hr. a day.

2. Limit phone, video games or watching TV to 1 hr. a day.

Strategic Action Steps for Achieving this Goal	Begin date	Target Date	Completed date
1. Create flash cards and study at least 10 minutes a day.	10/10/17	5/31/18	5/10/18
2. Take better notes in class	10/12/17	5/31/18	5/31/18
3. Read the text book or other books for class for 15 min a day	10/20/17	5/31/18	5/31/18
4. Start a study group before each major test.	11/10/17	5/31/18	5/15/18
5. Improve grade to 84 by mid-year	10/1/17	1/15/18	1/10/18
6.			
7.			
8.			
9.			
10.			

What resources, skills and/or people do I need to accomplish this goal?
1. Study Group   6. Read other history material.
2. Flash Cards
3. Parents help and support
4. Review goal weekly to make sure on target.
5. Improve note taking.

Affirmations to support this goal:
1. I earn a 90 or above in history class at the end of the 2017 – 18 school year.
2. No one or nothing will stop me from achieving my goal.
3. I am focused and avoid any distractions to get the job done.

Is this goal worth the time, effort or money required? (Circle)	Yes	No	
Does this goal support my values? (Circle)	Yes	No	

Goals Matter! Planning Sheet

Goal: (specific, measurable, actionable, reinforcing and trackable)

Measures to success:

Term of Goal: ___ Short-Term (within 1 year) ___Med.-Term (within 3 years) _____Long-Term (Over 3 Years)

Life Area (circle one): Spiritual– Relational – Physical– Social - Financial– Mental - Professional

Begin Date: _____Target Completion Date: _____

Actual Completion Date:_____

Possible opportunities for success: (What will you get from accomplishing this goal?)

Barriers to success: (Things that can prohibit you from achieving this goal.)

New habit(s): (What new daily habits can you implement to make this goal a reality?)

Strategic Action Steps for Achieving this Goal	Begin date	Target Date	Completed date

What resources, skills and/or people do I need to accomplish this goal?

Affirmations to support this goal:

Is this goal worth the time, effort or money required? (Circle)	Yes	No
Does this goal support my values? (Circle)	Yes	No

Goals Matter! Planning Sheet

Goal: (specific, measurable, actionable, reinforcing and trackable)

Measures to success:

Term of Goal: ___ Short-Term (within 1 year) ___Med.-Term (within 3 years) _____Long-Term (Over 3 Years)

Life Area (circle one): Spiritual– Relational – Physical– Social - Financial– Mental - Professional

Begin Date: _____Target Completion Date: _____

Actual Completion Date:_____

Possible opportunities for success: (What will you get from accomplishing this goal?)

Barriers to success: (Things that can prohibit you from achieving this goal.)

New habit(s): (What new daily habits can you implement to make this goal a reality?)

Strategic Action Steps for Achieving this Goal	Begin date	Target Date	Completed date

What resources, skills and/or people do I need to accomplish this goal?

Affirmations to support this goal:

Is this goal worth the time, effort or money required? (Circle)	Yes	No
Does this goal support my values? (Circle)	Yes	No

Goals Matter! Planning Sheet

Goal: (specific, measurable, actionable, reinforcing and trackable)

Measures to success:

Term of Goal: ___ Short-Term (within 1 year) ___Med.-Term (within 3 years) _____Long-Term (Over 3 Years)

Life Area (circle one): Spiritual– Relational – Physical– Social - Financial– Mental - Professional
Begin Date: _____Target Completion Date: _____
Actual Completion Date:_____

Possible opportunities for success: (What will you get from accomplishing this goal?)

Barriers to success: (Things that can prohibit you from achieving this goal.)

New habit(s): (What new daily habits can you implement to make this goal a reality?)

Strategic Action Steps for Achieving this Goal	Begin date	Target Date	Completed date

What resources, skills and/or people do I need to accomplish this goal?

Affirmations to support this goal:

Is this goal worth the time, effort or money required? (Circle)	Yes	No
Does this goal support my values? (Circle)	Yes	No

The Final Word

Work Your Plan

Work Your Plan

"An ounce of action is worth a ton of theory." Ralph Waldo Emerson

Now that you understand more about your purpose, and you have listed your core values, set some goals and described what you would like in the future, it is time to work your plan. It is great to have a well-written plan that you and others can see and reference, but it does you no good to have a well-written plan and not take action. You cannot afford to sit back and wait and think that you are going to take a free ride to living your best life. You must work your plan.

Stop talking and take action

Your dreams are waiting for you to live them. There are enough dead dreams in the graveyard. Graveyards are full of dreams that never were fulfilled because people kept talking about their dreams instead of living them.

"Whatever course you decide upon, there is always someone to tell you that you are wrong. There are always difficulties arising which tempt you to believe that your critics are right. To map out a course of action and follow it to an end requires courage." Ralph Waldo Emerson

There are dreams that you must release from your life. If you do not, yours will be another casualty in the graveyard of dead dreams. If you have made it this far then you are serious about chasing your dreams. If you do not live your dreams, they will never be lived.

If you have a book inside you, write it and let the world read it. If you have a song, sing it so others can hear it. If you have a business, develop the plan and implement it to help others. If you have a testimony about overcoming a tough situation, share it so others will be changed. You are never too old or young.

It is only when you stop talking about what you want to do and take action that you will begin to see your dreams unfold. Your life will grow. Your relationships will prosper. Your thoughts will expand. Your opportunities will multiply. Your health will improve. Whatever is in you, let it shine through your actions and not your words.

In working on your dreams, you will run into opposition and obstacles that will try to make you quit and give up. They will come at you daily with negative thoughts and words of failure, but you must keep your eyes on the prize.

Break free from the familiar

Many young people complain about the way things are and the direction their lives are going, but they are reluctant to make even the smallest adjustments to change their course. Instead of making the necessary adjustments, they would rather live in a comfort zone.

You were created with unique gifts and talents to present to the world. You have uniqueness to stand out and not blend in. We often miss doing great things because we spend too much time fitting in rather than standing out.

Many young people blend in rather than stand out because they fear the work, and possible ridicule, involved. Standing out forces you to break free from the

> **"Always be a first rate version of yourself instead of a second rate version of somebody else." Judy Garland**

familiar and live differently. Blending in keeps you locked in the familiar. Standing out will put you in uncomfortable situations that allow you to express your uniqueness. Blending in will cause you to miss living your best life because you want to stay comfortable.

A comfort zone is a mental state in which you lose the momentum to pursue a dream or goal because you have accepted where you are as the best you need to be or do.

You must fight through the temptations to settle in your comfort zone. You must overcome the desires to procrastinate. You cannot be lazy and slothful. You have a dream to work through.

Will you be satisfied if your tomorrow looks exactly like your today? If nothing changes in the next few months, will you feel like you have made significant progress toward discovering and living your dreams and goals? Are you on the right path headed in the right direction or are you wasting time and energy on the wrong path going in circles?

> **"If you spend too much time thinking about a thing, you'll never get it done." Bruce Lee**

You can be certain of one thing: your life will not progress unless you decide that it is going to be different. You are not a victim; you are a unique person designed for a specific purpose. Where you have been is just preparation for where you are going. If you want to pursue your dreams in full effect, choose to work your plan today.

Don't worry if everything does not happen as fast as you want. Don't throw in the towel if you do not get support from the people you thought would support you. Don't think doing things differently won't work today because you failed yesterday. The choice is yours whether you live life differently or you keep living the same! Work your plan and see what happens!

"The price of success is hard work, dedication to the job at hand and the determination that, whether we win or lose, we have applied the best of ourselves to the task at hand." Vince Lombardi

Appendixes

Appendix A – Form to write your vision statement

Write Your Vision

Now is the time to write your vision statement. A vision statement will help raise a thirst and hunger in you like never before. What you write down may not match your current situation. What you write down may seem unachievable. What you write down may look crazy to others and even you.

Your written vision statement is your plan to put into action. As you take action on your vision, you will need to continually monitor your progress to see where you

> *"Every man is born into the world to do something unique and something distinctive and if he does not do it, it will never be done." Benjamin E. Mays*

are and if you are on the right path. Examining your vision process regularly lets you know if you need to make any adjustments or changes.

Once you write it down the way you like, type it on one page and frame it. Just as a business or organization posts its vision statement, I encourage you to post your framed vision statement in a visible location in your home, on your phone, tablet, or computer so that you are reminded daily of your specific vision.

You cannot make your vision a reality on your own. You will need some help. Enlist the help of those who are willing to encourage and walk with you, even when things do not make sense and they cannot see the reality of your vision. Disassociate with anything or anyone that is an obstacle to where you want to go. You must diffuse the distractions immediately because they can cause you to forfeit your vision with negative and discouraging talk and actions.

On the following form, draft your personal vision statement. Once you have a written vision statement you are happy with, post it and start living it.

"Where there is no vision the people perish…." Proverbs 29:18

_____Vision Statement
(Your Name)

Write your purpose statement. (See Chapter 7, "In Position for Purpose")

Write your values in prioritize order. (See Chapter 8, "Your Values Count")

How do you see your Future? (Spiritual, Relational, Physical, Mental, Social, Financial, Professional) (See Chapter 9, "Vision Impact")

Brandon Jones
Personal Vision Statement

Purpose:

I help bring out the color within people's lives by encouraging, equipping and empowering them to dance to their music and live life at maximum capacity.

My Core Values:

1. Growing Relationship with God
2. Respecting my parents
3. Living out my uniqueness
4. Encouraging Family and Friends
5. Excellent Physical Health
6. Daily Peace of Mind
7. Financial Freedom
8. Continual Personal Development
9. Enjoy Life

Seeing My Future (Vision):

- I have daily fellowship with God that helps me grow in all aspects of my life.

- I love, honor and respect my parents so that we have a solid and lasting bond forever.

- I am a role model for young people and adults so they have a solid blueprint on what it takes to be an effective and productive person.

- I speak and/or listen to positive and affirmative words over my life every morning, afternoon and evening to help strengthen my mind against the negative and pessimistic words of others.

- I own and lead a successful multi-million business that help people live out their vision.

- I make wise investments and spending decisions at a young age so that I am able to live debt free, leave a financial generation inheritance, travel, bless others and live the lifestyle of my choice.

- I live a healthy lifestyle that keeps my mind at peace, gives me energy to live out my vision, maintains my ideal body weight, allows me to participate in recreational activities and live disease free.